Made from scratch

BAKING

EVERYDAY EASY HOME COOKING

This edition published by Parragon Books Ltd in 2014
and distributed by

Parragon Inc.
440 Park Avenue South, 13th Floor
New York, NY 10016
www.parragon.com/lovefood

LOVE FOOD is an imprint of Parragon Books Ltd

ISBN 978-1-4723-2996-7

Printed in China

Additional text by Angela Drake
Cover photography by Ian Garlick
New photography by Clive Streeter
New food styling by Angela Drake and Sally Streeter
Nutritional analysis by Fiona Hunter

Notes for the Reader
This book uses standard kitchen measuring spoons and cups. All spoon and
cup measurements are level unless otherwise indicated. Unless otherwise
stated, milk is assumed to be whole, eggs are large, individual vegetables are
medium, and pepper is freshly ground black pepper. Unless otherwise stated,
all root vegetables should be peeled prior to using.

Garnishes, decorations, and serving suggestions are all optional and not
necessarily included in the recipe ingredients or method. Any optional
ingredients and seasoning to taste are not included in the nutritional analysis.
The times given are only an approximate guide. Preparation times differ
according to the techniques used by different people and the cooking times
may also vary from those given. Optional ingredients, variations, or serving
suggestions have not been included in the time calculations.

Contents

Introduction

There's something extra special about a homemade cake. While it may not have the perfectly proportioned features of a store-bought version, the flavor will almost certainly be far superior and you'll also know exactly what went into it! Home baking has never been so popular.

This book is the perfect choice for novice cooks wanting to learn the basics of home baking, but it's also ideal for more experienced cooks who will find a whole variety of new and original ideas to broaden their repertoire. Included are recipes ranging from cupcakes, muffins, and cookies to classic cakes, tarts, breads, pies, and desserts—some can easily be made in minutes, others will take longer and require a little more skill and patience.

It is worth buying good-quality equipment that will last—if you like baking cupcakes, then invest in a good muffin pan. If you only make layer cakes occasionally, it is probably best to borrow cake pans from a friend. Whatever you choose to bake, the finest quality ingredients will always give the best flavor.

Each recipe has clear and easy to understand numbered instructions and simple step-by-step pictures to guide you. The book is also full of useful hints and tips, from freezing information to time-saving techniques and flavor variations.

Secrets of successful baking

- Prepare the kitchen before you start by clearing work surfaces and making sure you have enough space to work in.

- Check that you have all the ingredients to make the recipe—you don't want to run out of something at a crucial moment.

- Make sure that the cake pan is the correct size and prepare by greasing and/or lining.

- Preheat the oven to the required temperature and take eggs out of the refrigerator at least one hour before starting. If the recipe requires softened butter, let it stand at room temperature for about an hour.

- For bread making, a warm kitchen will help the dough to rise so turn the oven on earlier than needed.

There is nothing more satisfying than creating delicious homemade goodies for family and friends.

- For pastry making, keep hands and equipment as cool as possible to prevent the fat from melting and making the pastry sticky.

- Always measure ingredients carefully and use measuring spoons for raising agents and flavorings.

- Don't be tempted to open the oven door too early—a blast of cold air can soon make a cake sink!

- To check if a sponge cake is ready, gently press the surface with your fingertips. It should spring back without leaving an impression. For deeper cakes or rich fruitcakes, check by inserting a skewer into the center of the cake—it should come out clean.

- To check if bread is ready, hold the loaf with a thick dish towel and tap the base firmly with your knuckles—it should sound hollow.

- Leave cakes and bakes to cool completely before storing in airtight plastic containers.

Classic Chocolate Cake *8*

Red Velvet Cake *10*

Coffee & Walnut Cake *12*

Rich Fruitcake *14*

Pumpkin Spice Cake *16*

Coconut Layer Cake *18*

Frosted Fruit Cake *20*

Strawberry Layer Cake *22*

White Chocolate Coffee Cake *24*

Coffee Bundt Cake *26*

Angel Food Cake *28*

Mini Carrot Cakes *30*

Apple Crumb Cake *32*

Maple & Pecan Bundt Cake *34*

Cakes

Classic Chocolate Cake

 SERVES 10   PREP TIME: 25 minutes plus chilling    COOKING TIME: 25–30 minutes

nutritional information per serving	581 cal, 41g fat, 25g sat fat, 32g total sugars, 0.7g salt

For sheer indulgence, nothing beats a slice of moist chocolate cake smothered in a rich and creamy frosting.

INGREDIENTS

⅔ cup unsweetened cocoa powder
½ cup boiling water
1¾ sticks salted butter, softened, plus extra for greasing
⅔ cup superfine sugar
⅓ cup firmly packed light brown sugar
4 eggs, beaten
1 teaspoon vanilla extract
1⅔ cups all-purpose flour
2¼ teaspoons baking powder

frosting

7 ounces semisweet chocolate, broken into pieces
1 stick unsalted butter
½ cup heavy cream

1. Preheat the oven to 350°F. Grease two 8-inch cake pans and line with parchment paper.

2. Blend the cocoa powder and water to a smooth paste and set aside. Put the butter, superfine sugar, and brown sugar into a large bowl and beat together until pale and creamy. Gradually beat in the eggs, then stir in the cocoa paste and vanilla extract.

3. Sift in the flour and baking powder and fold in gently. Divide the batter between the prepared pans. Bake in the preheated oven for 25–30 minutes, or until risen and just springy to the touch. Let cool in the pans for 5 minutes, then invert onto a wire rack to cool completely.

4. To make the frosting, put the chocolate and butter into a heatproof bowl set over a saucepan of simmering water and heat until melted. Remove from the heat and stir in the cream. Let cool for 20 minutes, then chill in the refrigerator for 40–50 minutes, stirring occasionally, until thick enough to spread.

5. Sandwich the sponges together with one-third of the frosting, then spread the remainder over the top and sides of the cake.

Red Velvet Cake

 SERVES 12

 PREP TIME:
25 minutes
plus cooling

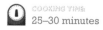 COOKING TIME:
25–30 minutes

nutritional information per serving	510 cal, 32g fat, 20g sat fat, 28g total sugars, 0.5g salt

A popular cake with a rich buttermilk-flavored chocolate sponge, it is colored deep red by edible food coloring and topped off with a traditional vanilla cream cheese frosting.

INGREDIENTS

2 sticks unsalted butter, plus extra for greasing
¼ cup water
⅔ cup unsweetened cocoa powder
3 eggs, beaten
1 cup buttermilk
2 teaspoons vanilla extract
2 tablespoons red food coloring
2¼ cups all-purpose flour
½ cup cornstarch
1½ teaspoons baking powder
1⅓ cups superfine sugar

frosting
1 cup cream cheese
3 tablespoons unsalted butter
3 tablespoons superfine sugar
1 teaspoon vanilla extract

1. Preheat the oven to 375°F. Grease two 9-inch cake pans and line with parchment paper.

2. Place the butter, water, and cocoa powder in a small saucepan and heat gently, without boiling, stirring until melted and smooth. Remove from the heat and let cool slightly.

3. Beat together the eggs, buttermilk, vanilla extract, and food coloring in a bowl until frothy. Beat in the butter mixture. Sift together the flour, cornstarch, and baking powder, then stir quickly and evenly into the mixture with the superfine sugar.

4. Divide the batter between the prepared pans and bake in the preheated oven for 25–30 minutes, or until risen and firm to the touch. Let cool in the pans for 3–4 minutes, then invert onto a wire rack to cool completely.

5. To make the frosting, beat together all the ingredients until smooth. Use about half of the frosting to sandwich together the cakes, then spread the remainder over the top, swirling with a spatula.

Coffee & Walnut Cake

 SERVES 8

 PREP TIME:
30 minutes
plus cooling

 COOKING TIME
20–25 minutes

nutritional information
per serving   667 cal, 44g fat, 22g sat fat, 46g total sugars, 0.5g salt

Coffee and walnuts complement each other perfectly in this much-loved layer cake.

INGREDIENTS

1½ sticks unsalted butter, softened, plus extra for greasing
¾ cup firmly packed light brown sugar
3 extra-large eggs, beaten
3 tablespoons strong black coffee
1⅓ cups all-purpose flour
3½ teaspoons baking powder
1 cup walnut pieces
walnut halves, to decorate

frosting
1 stick unsalted butter, softened
1⅔ cups confectioners' sugar
1 tablespoon strong black coffee
½ teaspoon vanilla extract

1. Preheat the oven to 350°F. Grease two 8-inch cake pans and line with parchment paper.

2. Beat together the butter and brown sugar until pale and creamy. Gradually add the eggs, beating well after each addition. Beat in the coffee.

3. Sift the flour and baking powder into the mixture, then fold in lightly and evenly with a metal spoon. Fold in the walnut pieces. Divide the batter between the prepared cake pans and smooth the surfaces. Bake in the preheated oven for 20–25 minutes, or until golden brown and springy to the touch. Invert onto a wire rack to cool completely.

4. To make the frosting, beat together the butter, confectioners' sugar, coffee, and vanilla extract, mixing until smooth and creamy.

5. Use about half the mixture to sandwich the cakes together, then spread the remaining frosting on top and swirl with a spatula. Decorate with walnut halves.

2

3

5

Rich Fruitcake

 SERVES 16   PREP TIME 30 minutes plus soaking/storing   COOKING TIME 2¼–2¾ hours

nutritional information per serving	400 cal, 16g fat, 8.5g sat fat, 49g total sugars, 0.15g salt

The cake of choice for a traditional Christmas celebration, this classic favorite should be made well in advance to allow time for the rich flavors to mature.

INGREDIENTS

2⅓ cups golden raisins

1½ cups raisins

¾ cup chopped dried apricots

⅔ cup chopped pitted dates

¼ cup dark rum or brandy, plus extra for flavoring (optional)

finely grated rind and juice of 1 orange

2 sticks unsalted butter, softened, plus extra for greasing

1 cup firmly packed light brown sugar

4 eggs, beaten

⅓ cup chopped candied peel

⅓ cup quartered candied cherries

2 pieces chopped candied ginger or preserved ginger

¼ cup blanched almonds, chopped

1⅔ cups all-purpose flour

1 teaspoon ground allspice

1. Place the golden raisins, raisins, apricots, and dates in a large bowl and stir in the rum, if using, orange rind, and orange juice. Cover and let soak for several hours or overnight.

2. Preheat the oven to 300°F. Grease an 8-inch round cake pan and line with parchment paper.

3. Beat together the butter and sugar in a large mixing bowl until pale and creamy. Gradually beat in the eggs, beating hard after each addition. Stir in the soaked fruits, candied peel, candied cherries, candied ginger, and blanched almonds.

4. Sift the flour and allspice over the beaten mixture, then fold in lightly and evenly. Spoon the batter into the prepared cake pan and smooth the surface, making a slight depression in the center with the back of the spoon.

5. Bake in the preheated oven for 2¼–2¾ hours, or until the cake begins to shrink away from the sides and a toothpick inserted into the center comes out clean. Cool completely in the pan.

6. Invert the cake and remove the parchment paper. Wrap in some wax paper and aluminum foil, and store for at least two months before use. To add a richer flavor, prick the cake with a toothpick and spoon over a couple of extra tablespoons of rum or brandy, if using, before storing.

Pumpkin Spice Cake

 SERVES 8

 PREP TIME
25 minutes
plus cooling

 COOKING TIME
35–40 minutes

nutritional information per serving	631 cal, 39g fat, 12g sat fat, 44g total sugars, 0.9g salt

This lightly spiced fruit and nut cake is smothered with a rich and creamy maple syrup frosting.

INGREDIENTS

¾ cup sunflower oil, plus extra for greasing
¾ cup packed light brown sugar
3 eggs, beaten
1 cup canned pumpkin puree
⅔ cup raisins
grated rind of 1 orange
⅔ cup walnut pieces
1¾ cups all-purpose flour
1 teaspoon baking soda
2¾ teaspoons baking powder
2 teaspoons allspice

frosting

1 cup mascarpone cheese
⅔ cup confectioners' sugar
3 tablespoons maple syrup

1. Preheat the oven to 350°F. Grease a 9-inch square cake pan and line with parchment paper.

2. In a large bowl, beat together the oil, brown sugar, and eggs. Stir in the pumpkin puree, raisins, orange rind, and ½ cup of the walnut pieces.

3. Sift together the flour, baking soda, baking powder, and allspice and fold into the pumpkin mixture. Spoon the batter into the prepared pan and bake in the preheated oven for 35–40 minutes, or until golden brown and firm to the touch. Let cool in the pan for 5 minutes, then invert onto a wire rack to cool completely.

4. To make the frosting, put the mascarpone cheese, confectioners' sugar, and maple syrup into a bowl and beat together until smooth. Spread over the top of the cake, swirling with a spatula. Finely chop the remaining walnut pieces and sprinkle over the top of the cake.

2

3

4

HEALTHY HINT
For a lighter frosting, use thick Greek-style yogurt sweetened to taste with honey. Spread over the cake just before serving.

Coconut Layer Cake

 SERVES 8

 PREP TIME:
30 minutes
plus cooling

 COOKING TIME:
20–25 minutes

nutritional information per serving	592 cal, 42g fat, 26g sat fat, 28g total sugars, 0.35g salt

This cake is perfect for a special occasion with light-as-air coconut sponge filled and covered with a divinely creamy, smooth frosting.

INGREDIENTS

6 extra-large eggs, beaten

¾ cup plus 2 tablespoons superfine sugar

1⅓ cup plus 1 tablespoon all-purpose flour

1 cup dry unsweetened coconut

4 tablespoons salted butter, melted and cooled, plus extra for greasing

toasted coconut shavings, to decorate

frosting
1 cup mascarpone cheese

¼ cup coconut milk

2 tablespoons superfine sugar

⅔ cup heavy cream

1. Preheat the oven to 350°F. Grease three 8-inch round cake pans and line with parchment paper.

2. Put the eggs and sugar into a large, heatproof bowl set over a saucepan of simmering water. Beat with an electric handheld mixer until the mixture is thick and pale and leaves a trail when the beaters are lifted.

3. Sift half of the flour over the beaten mixture and gently fold in, then sift the rest of the flour over the mixture and fold in again. Fold in the coconut. Pour the butter in a thin stream over the mixture and fold in until just incorporated.

4. Divide the batter between the prepared pans and bake in the preheated oven for 20–25 minutes, or until light golden and springy to the touch. Let cool in the pans for 5 minutes, then invert onto a wire rack to cool completely.

5. To make the frosting, put the mascarpone cheese, coconut milk, and sugar into a bowl and beat together until smooth. Whip the cream until it holds soft peaks, then fold it into the mixture.

6. Sandwich the sponges together with one-third of the frosting and spread the remainder over the top and sides of the cake. Decorate with coconut shavings.

Frosted Fruit Cake

 SERVES 16

 PREP TIME: 50 minutes plus chilling

 COOKING TIME: 35–40 minutes

nutritional information per serving	502 cal, 33g fat, 20g sat fat, 35g total sugars, 0.6g salt

This impressive cake is perfect for a summer afternoon get-together or as a dessert after a leisurely lunch. Use firm, undamaged fruit so that their juices don't seep into the frosting.

INGREDIENTS

2½ sticks salted butter, softened, plus extra for greasing
2⅓ cups superfine sugar
5 eggs, beaten
1 tablespoon vanilla extract
2¼ cups all-purpose flour
1 tablespoon baking powder
3 tablespoons milk
⅓ cup raspberry preserves or strawberry preserves
⅔ cup heavy cream
about 3 cups mixed berries, such as strawberries, raspberries, and blueberries
confectioners' sugar, for sprinkling

frosting
1 cup cream cheese
1 stick unsalted butter, softened
1 teaspoon lemon juice
1 cup confectioners' sugar
pink food coloring

1. Preheat the oven to 350°F. Grease two 8-inch cake pans and line with parchment paper. Put the butter and superfine sugar into a bowl and beat together until pale and creamy. Gradually beat in the eggs, then stir in the vanilla extract. Sift in the flour and baking powder and fold in gently. Stir in the milk. Divide the batter between the prepared pans. Bake in the preheated oven for 35–40 minutes, or until springy to the touch. Invert onto a wire rack to cool.

2. Place one of the cakes on a flat serving plate and spread with the preserves. Whip the cream until it is just holding its shape. Spread the cream over the preserves, almost to the edges of the cake. Position the second cake on top and press down gently so the cream is level with the edges of the cake.

3. To make the frosting, beat together the cream cheese and butter. Add the lemon juice and confectioners' sugar and beat until light and creamy. Beat a dash of pink food coloring into the frosting to color it the palest shade of pink. Using a spatula, spread a thin layer over the top and sides of the cake to seal in the crumbs. The cake will still show through at this stage, but it will be covered by the second layer of frosting. Chill in the refrigerator for 15 minutes.

4. Use the spatula to spread a thicker layer of frosting around the sides of the cake. Spread the remainder over the top. Once evenly covered, use the edge of the spatula to swirl the frosting as smoothly or as textured as you desire. Arrange the fruits on top of the cake. Put a little confectioners' sugar in a small, fine strainer and gently tap it over the fruits to lightly frost.

3

4

4

Strawberry Layer Cake

 SERVES 8

 PREP TIME:
30 minutes
plus cooling

 COOKING TIME:
25–30 minutes

nutritional information
per serving | 566 cal, 42g fat, 25g sat fat, 28g total sugars, 0.8g salt

This classic layer cake is given the star treatment with a luxurious filling of preserves, softly whipped cream, and fresh strawberries. Just perfect for a summer afternoon coffee break.

INGREDIENTS

1⅓ cups all-purpose flour
2¾ teaspoons baking powder
1½ sticks salted butter, softened, plus extra for greasing
1 cup superfine sugar
3 eggs, beaten
confectioners' sugar, for dusting

filling
3 tablespoons raspberry preserves
1¼ cups heavy cream, whipped
16 fresh strawberries, halved

1. Preheat the oven to 350°F. Grease two 8-inch cake pans and line with parchment paper.

2. Sift the flour and baking powder into a bowl and add the butter, sugar, and eggs. Mix together, then beat well until smooth.

3. Divide the batter evenly between the prepared pans and smooth the surfaces. Bake in the preheated oven for 25–30 minutes, or until well risen and golden brown, and the cakes feel springy when lightly pressed.

4. Let cool in the pans for 5 minutes, then invert and peel off the parchment paper. Transfer to wire racks to cool completely. Sandwich the cakes together with the raspberry preserves, whipped cream, and strawberry halves. Dust with confectioners' sugar.

2

3

4

White Chocolate Coffee Cake

 SERVES 10

 PREP TIME:
30 minutes
plus chilling

 COOKING TIME:
25–30 minutes

nutritional information per serving	467 cal, 27g fat, 16g sat fat, 40g total sugars, 0.2g salt

This coffee-flavored cake has a wonderful smooth and tangy crème fraîche and white chocolate frosting.

INGREDIENTS

3 tablespoons unsalted butter, plus extra for greasing
3 ounces white chocolate, broken into pieces
⅔ cup superfine sugar
4 extra-large eggs, beaten
2 tablespoons strong black coffee
1 teaspoon vanilla extract
1 cup all-purpose flour

frosting

6 ounces white chocolate
6 tablespoons unsalted butter
½ cup crème fraîche
1 cup confectioners' sugar, sifted
1 tablespoon coffee liqueur

1. Preheat the oven to 350°F. Grease two 8-inch cake pans and line with parchment paper. Place the butter and chocolate in a heatproof bowl set over a saucepan of gently simmering water and heat until melted. Stir to mix, then remove from the heat. Place the superfine sugar, eggs, coffee, and vanilla in a heatproof bowl set over a saucepan of hot water and beat until the batter leaves a trail when the beaters or whisk are lifted. Remove from the heat, sift in the flour, and mix in lightly and evenly. Quickly stir in the butter-and-chocolate mixture, then divide the batter between the prepared pans. Bake in the preheated oven for 25–30 minutes, until risen, golden brown, and springy to the touch. Let cool in the pans for 2 minutes, then invert onto a wire rack.

2. To make the frosting, put the chocolate and butter in a heatproof bowl set over a saucepan of gently simmering water and heat until melted. Remove from the heat, stir in the crème fraîche, add the confectioners' sugar and coffee liqueur, and mix. Chill until thick. Sandwich the cakes together with a third of the frosting, then spread the rest over the cake.

1

1

2

COOK'S NOTE
Be careful when melting white chocolate because it can turn grainy if overheated.

Coffee Bundt Cake

 SERVES 14   PREP TIME: 40 minutes plus cooling   COOKING TIME: 50 minutes

nutritional information per serving	505 cal, 28g fat, 17g sat fat, 36g total sugars, 0.9g salt

Bundt cakes cook quickly and, therefore, stay deliciously moist, because of the hole through the center of the pan.

INGREDIENTS

3¼ cups all-purpose flour, plus extra for dusting

1 tablespoon baking powder

1 teaspoon baking soda

3 tablespoons espresso coffee powder

2½ sticks salted butter, softened, plus extra for greasing

½ cup firmly packed light brown sugar

1 cup maple syrup

3 eggs, beaten

1 cup buttermilk

1 cup heavy cream

decoration

¼ cup maple syrup

1⅔ cups confectioners' sugar

1 tablespoon unsalted butter, melted

20 chocolate-coated coffee beans

1. Preheat the oven to 350°F. Grease and lightly flour a 3-quart bundt cake pan.

2. Sift the flour, baking powder, baking soda, and coffee powder into a bowl. In a separate bowl, beat together the butter and brown sugar until pale and creamy. Gradually beat in the maple syrup. Beat in the eggs slowly, adding 3 tablespoons of the flour mixture to prevent it from curdling.

3. Mix together the buttermilk and cream and add half to the butter mixture. Sprinkle in half of the flour mixture and fold together gently. Add the remaining buttermilk and flour mixtures and mix together gently until just combined.

4. Spoon the batter into the prepared pan and smooth the surface. Bake in the preheated oven for about 50 minutes, or until well risen and a toothpick inserted into the center comes out clean. Let stand in the pan for 10 minutes, then loosen with a knife and invert onto a wire rack to cool completely.

5. To decorate, beat the maple syrup in a bowl with 1¼ cups of the confectioners' sugar and the butter, until smooth and thickly coating the back of a wooden spoon. Transfer the cake to a serving plate and spoon the icing around the top of the cake so it starts to run down the sides.

6. Beat the remaining confectioners' sugar in a small bowl with 1½–2 teaspoons of water to make a smooth paste. Using a teaspoon, drizzle the icing over the cake. Spread the coffee beans over the top.

5

6

Angel Food Cake

 SERVES 10   PREP TIME: 30 minutes plus cooling    COOKING TIME: 40–45 minutes

nutritional information
per serving   171 cal, 0.5g fat, 0.1g sat fat, 29g total sugars, 0.13g salt

This light fat-free sponge cake is topped with fresh berries and makes a great dessert for a summer barbecue or alfresco meal.

INGREDIENTS

sunflower oil, for greasing

8 extra-large egg whites

1 teaspoon cream of tartar

1 teaspoon almond extract

1¼ cups superfine sugar

1 cup all-purpose flour, plus extra for dusting

decoration

2 cups mixed berries, such as raspberries, strawberries and blueberries

1 tablespoon lemon juice

2 tablespoons confectioners' sugar

1. Preheat the oven to 325°F. Grease and lightly flour a 9-inch tube pan.

2. In a clean, grease-free bowl, beat the egg whites until they hold soft peaks. Add the cream of tartar and beat again until the whites are stiff but not dry. Beat in the almond extract, then add the superfine sugar, a tablespoon at a time, beating hard between each addition. Sift in the flour and fold in lightly and evenly, using a large metal spoon.

3. Spoon the batter into the prepared cake pan. Bake in the preheated oven for 40–45 minutes, or until golden brown. Run the tip of a knife around the edges of the cake to loosen from the pan. Let cool in the pan for 10 minutes, then invert onto a wire rack to cool.

4. To decorate, place the berries, lemon juice, and confectioners' sugar in a saucepan and heat until the sugar has dissolved. Spoon over the top of the cake.

2

2

3

GOES WELL WITH
Serve this
delicious cake
with whipped
heavy cream
sweetened with a
little confectioners'
sugar.

Mini Carrot Cakes

 MAKES 20

 PREP TIME:
1 hour
plus cooling

 COOKING TIME:
35 minutes

nutritional information per cake	250 cal, 15.5g fat, 8g sat fat, 19g total sugars, 0.32g salt

Carrot cake is such an all-time favorite, it had to be included here. If you're making these in advance, the little marzipan carrots can be positioned after frosting the cake.

INGREDIENTS

1¼ sticks salted butter, softened, plus extra for greasing

¾ cup firmly packed light brown sugar

3 eggs, beaten

1¼ cups all-purpose flour

2 teaspoons baking powder

½ teaspoon ground allspice

1 cup almond meal (ground almonds)

finely grated rind of 1 lemon

1⅓ cups shredded carrots

½ cup coarsely chopped golden raisins

decoration

⅔ cup cream cheese

3 tablespoons unsalted butter, softened

1 cup confectioners' sugar, plus extra for dusting

2 tablespoons lemon juice

2¼ ounces marzipan

orange food coloring

several sprigs of dill

1. Preheat the oven to 350°F. Grease a 10-inch x 8-inch baking pan and line with parchment paper. Grease the parchment paper. Put the butter, light brown sugar, eggs, flour, baking powder, allspice, almond meal, and lemon rind in a mixing bowl and beat together with an electric handheld mixer until smooth and creamy. Stir in the carrots and golden raisins.

2. Spoon the batter into the prepared pan and smooth the surface. Bake in the preheated oven for 35 minutes, or until risen and just firm to the touch. Let cool in the pan for 10 minutes, then transfer to a wire rack to cool.

3. For the decoration, beat together the cream cheese, butter, confectioners' sugar, and lemon juice until creamy. Color the marzipan deep orange by dabbing a few drops of the food coloring onto the marzipan and rolling out the marzipan on a surface lightly dusted with confectioners' sugar until the color is evenly mixed. Roll the marzipan into a sausage shape, then divide it into 20 pieces and form each one into a small carrot shape, marking shallow grooves around each with a knife.

4. Using a spatula, spread the frosting over the cake, taking it almost to the edges. Trim the crusts from the cake to neaten it, then cut it into 20 squares. Place a marzipan carrot on each cake and add a small sprig of dill to each one.

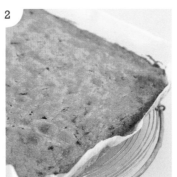

Apple Crumb Cake

 SERVES 10

 PREP TIME:
30 minutes
plus chilling

 COOKING TIME:
1 hour, 20 mins

nutritional information per serving	451 cal, 26g fat, 13g sat fat, 28g total sugars, 0.7g salt

Chunks of moist apple in a spiced sponge, topped off with a deliciously nutty crumb crust—irresistible!

INGREDIENTS

1½ sticks salted butter, softened, plus extra for greasing
1 cup superfine sugar
3 extra-large eggs, beaten
2 tablespoons milk
1¾ cups all-purpose flour
2½ teaspoons baking powder
1 teaspoon ground cinnamon
½ teaspoon grated nutmeg
2 cooking apples (1 pound), such as Granny Smith or Pippin, peeled, cored, and chopped
ice cream or crème fraîche, to serve

crumb topping

¾ cup all-purpose flour
4 tablespoons salted butter, chilled and diced
¼ cup raw brown sugar
⅓ cup blanched hazelnuts, chopped

1. Preheat the oven to 350°F. Grease a 9-inch round springform cake pan and line with parchment paper.

2. Put the butter and superfine sugar into a large bowl and beat together until pale and fluffy, then gradually beat in the eggs. Stir in the milk. Sift together the flour, baking powder, and spices and gently fold in until thoroughly incorporated.

3. Spoon half the batter into the prepared pan and spread half the apples over the batter. Spoon over the remaining batter and spread evenly. Top with the remaining apples.

4. To make the crumb topping, sift the flour into a bowl, then add the butter and rub in until the mixture resembles bread crumbs. Stir in the raw brown sugar and nuts. Sprinkle the mixture evenly over the top of the cake.

5. Bake in the preheated oven for 1 hour, then cover loosely with aluminum foil to prevent the cake from overbrowning. Cook for an additional 10–20 minutes, or until golden brown and firm to the touch. Let cool in the pan for 20 minutes, then unclip the pan and carefully transfer to a wire rack. Serve warm or cold, with ice cream.

Maple & Pecan Bundt Cake

SERVES 10

 PREP TIME:
30 minutes
plus cooling

 COOKING TIME:
45–50 minutes

nutritional information
per serving · 466 cal, 28g fat, 14g sat fat, 33g total sugars, 0.6g salt

Baked in a classic fluted bundt cake pan, this cake looks and tastes amazing.

INGREDIENTS

1¾ sticks salted butter, softened, plus extra for greasing
1 cup firmly packed light brown sugar
3 extra-large eggs, beaten
½ cup finely chopped pecans
¼ cup maple syrup
⅔ cup sour cream
1¾ cups all-purpose flour, plus extra for dusting
2¾ teaspoons baking powder
chopped pecan nuts, to decorate

icing
⅔ cup confectioners' sugar, sifted
1 tablespoon maple syrup
1–2 tablespoons lukewarm water

1. Preheat the oven to 325°F. Grease and lightly flour a 2-quart bundt pan.

2. Put the butter and brown sugar into a bowl and beat together until pale and fluffy. Gradually beat in the eggs, then stir in the nuts, maple syrup, and sour cream. Sift in the flour and baking powder and fold in thoroughly.

3. Spoon the batter into the prepared pan and gently smooth the surface. Bake in the preheated oven for 45–50 minutes, or until the cake is firm and golden and a toothpick inserted into the center comes out clean. Let cool in the pan for 10 minutes, then invert onto a wire rack to cool completely.

4. To make the icing, mix the confectioners' sugar, maple syrup, and enough water to make a smooth icing. Spoon the icing over the top of the cake, letting it run down the sides. Decorate with the chopped nuts and let set.

2

3

3

COOK'S NOTE
Before inverting the cake out of the pan, gently loosen the edges from the sides with the tip of a thin spatula.

Classic Vanilla Cupcakes *38*

Berry Muffins *40*

White Chocolate & Raspberry Muffins *42*

Ultimate Chocolate Cupcakes *44*

Chocolate Chip Muffins *46*

Frosted Berry Cupcakes *48*

Hummingbird Cupcakes *50*

Chocolate & Orange Muffins *52*

Apple & Cinnamon Muffins *54*

Tiramisu Cupcakes *56*

Blueberry Muffins *58*

Candy Cupcakes *60*

Fudge Nut Muffins *62*

Apple Streusel Cupcakes *64*

Cupcakes & Muffins

Classic Vanilla Cupcakes

MAKES 12

PREP TIME
25 minutes

COOKING TIME
15–20 minutes

nutritional information
per cupcake   453 cal, 27g fat, 17g sat fat, 40g total sugars, 0.2g salt

Everyone's favorite—light and fluffy vanilla sponges topped with generous swirls of buttercream.

INGREDIENTS

1½ sticks unsalted butter, softened
1 cup superfine sugar
3 extra-large eggs, beaten
1 teaspoon vanilla extract
1⅓ cups all-purpose flour
2 teaspoons baking powder

frosting
1¼ sticks unsalted butter, softened
3 tablespoons heavy cream or whole milk
1 teaspoon vanilla extract
2⅓ cups confectioners' sugar, sifted
sprinkles, to decorate

1. Preheat the oven to 350°F. Place 12 muffin cups in a muffin pan.

2. Put the butter and superfine sugar into a bowl and beat together until pale and creamy. Gradually beat in the eggs and vanilla extract. Sift in the flour and baking powder and fold in gently.

3. Divide the batter evenly among the muffin cups and bake in the preheated oven for 15–20 minutes, or until risen and firm to the touch. Transfer to a wire rack and let cool.

4. To make the frosting, put the butter into a bowl and beat with an electric mixer for 2–3 minutes, or until pale and creamy. Beat in the cream and vanilla extract. Gradually beat in the confectioners' sugar and continue beating until the buttercream is light and fluffy.

5. Use a spatula to swirl the frosting over the tops of the cupcakes. Decorate with sprinkles.

SOMETHING
DIFFERENT
To make bite-size
cupcakes for children's
parties, divide the
batter among 30 mini
cupcake liners and
reduce the cooking
time to 8-10 minutes.

Berry Muffins

 MAKES 12   PREP TIME: 20 minutes   COOKING TIME: 20–25 minutes

nutritional information per muffin | 255 cal, 15g fat, 7g sat fat, 13g total sugars, 0.5g salt

Quick and easy to make, these muffins are packed full of fresh mixed berries.

INGREDIENTS

1¾ cups all-purpose flour

2 teaspoons baking powder

½ cup almond meal (ground almonds)

⅔ cup superfine sugar, plus extra for sprinkling

1¼ sticks salted butter, melted

½ cup milk

2 eggs, beaten

2 cups mixed berries, such as blueberries, raspberries, and blackberries

1. Preheat the oven to 375°F. Place 12 muffin cups in a muffin pan.

2. Sift together the flour and baking powder into a large bowl and stir in the almond meal and sugar. Make a well in the center of the dry ingredients.

3. Beat together the butter, milk, and eggs and pour into the well. Stir gently until just combined; do not overmix. Gently fold in the berries.

4. Divide the batter evenly among the muffin cups. Bake in the preheated oven for 20–25 minutes, or until light golden and just firm to the touch. Serve warm or cold, sprinkled with sugar.

2

3

4

White Chocolate & Raspberry Muffins

 MAKES 12    PREP TIME: 20 minutes   COOKING TIME: 20–25 minutes

nutritional information per muffin	246 cal, 11g fat, 6.5g sat fat, 18g total sugars, 0.5g salt

Best eaten warm from the oven, these muffins make a great mid morning snack.

INGREDIENTS

2 cups all-purpose flour
1 tablespoon baking powder
½ cup superfine sugar
6 tablespoons salted butter, chilled and coarsely grated
1 extra-large egg
¾ cup whole milk
1½ cups raspberries
¾ cup white chocolate chips

1. Preheat the oven to 400°F. Place 12 muffin cups in a muffin pan.

2. Sift together the flour and baking powder into a large bowl and stir in the sugar. Add the butter and stir with a fork to coat in the flour mixture. Lightly beat the egg in a bowl, then beat in the milk.

3. Make a well in the center of the dry ingredients and pour in the liquid ingredients. Stir gently until just combined; do not overmix. Fold in the raspberries and half of the chocolate chips.

4. Divide the batter evenly among the muffin cups and sprinkle the remaining chocolate chips over the muffins. Bake in the preheated oven for 20–25 minutes, or until risen, golden, and just firm to the touch. Let cool for 5 minutes, then transfer to a wire rack to cool completely.

SOMETHING
DIFFERENT
Replace the
raspberries with
fresh or frozen
blackberries,
or try chopped
fresh mango for
a tropical flavor.

Ultimate Chocolate Cupcakes

 MAKES 14 PREP TIME: 25 minutes plus chilling COOKING TIME: 15–20 minutes

nutritional information per cupcake	440 cal, 28g fat, 17g sat fat, 37g total sugars, 0.33g salt

Moist chocolate sponges topped with large swirls of rich and creamy frosting—these cupcakes are simply the best! Ideal for a special celebration or birthday because they can be made a day in advance.

INGREDIENTS

1 cup all-purpose flour
2 teaspoons baking powder
1½ tablespoons unsweetened cocoa powder
1 stick salted butter, softened, or ½ cup soft margarine
½ cup superfine sugar
2 extra-large eggs, beaten
2 ounces semisweet chocolate, melted

frosting
6 ounces semisweet chocolate, finely chopped
1 cup heavy cream
1¼ sticks unsalted butter, softened
2¼ cups confectioners' sugar, sifted
chocolate shapes and gold candied balls, to decorate (optional)

1. Preheat the oven to 350°F. Place 14 muffin cups in two muffin pans.

2. Sift the flour, baking powder, and cocoa powder into a large bowl. Add the butter, superfine sugar, and eggs and beat together until smooth. Fold in the melted chocolate.

3. Divide the batter evenly among the muffin cups. Bake in the preheated oven for 15–20 minutes, or until risen and firm to the touch. Transfer to a wire rack and let cool.

4. To make the frosting, put the chocolate in a heatproof bowl. Heat the cream in a saucepan until boiling, then pour over the chocolate and stir until smooth. Let cool, stirring occasionally, for 20 minutes, until thickened. Put the butter in a bowl, stir in the confectioners' sugar, and beat until smooth. Beat in the chocolate mixture. Chill for 15–20 minutes.

5. Spoon the frosting into a pastry bag fitted with a large star tip. Pipe swirls of frosting on top of each cupcake. Decorate with chocolate shapes and gold candied balls, if using.

Chocolate Chip Muffins

 MAKES 12   PREP TIME 20 minutes    COOKING TIME 20–25 minutes

nutritional information per muffin	252 cal, 11g fat, 6.5g sat fat, 15g total sugars, 0.6g salt

These classic American muffins have a lovely light texture and are full of delicious milk chocolate chunks.

INGREDIENTS

2⅓ cups all-purpose flour

5 teaspoons baking powder

6 tablespoons salted butter, chilled and diced

½ cup superfine sugar

6 ounces milk chocolate, chopped into chunks

2 extra-large eggs, beaten

1 cup buttermilk

1 teaspoon vanilla extract

1. Preheat the oven to 400°F. Place 12 muffin cups in a muffin pan.

2. Sift together the flour and baking powder into a large bowl. Add the butter and rub in to make fine bread crumbs. Stir in the sugar and the chocolate chunks.

3. Beat together the eggs, buttermilk, and vanilla extract. Make a well in the center of the dry ingredients and pour in the liquid ingredients. Stir gently until just combined; do not overmix.

4. Divide the batter evenly among the muffin cups. Bake in the preheated oven for 20–25 minutes, or until risen, golden, and just firm to the touch. Let cool for 5 minutes, then transfer to a wire rack to cool completely.

2

2

4

Frosted Berry Cupcakes

 MAKES 12

 PREP TIME: 25 minutes

 COOKING TIME: 15–20 minutes

nutritional information per cupcake	330 cal, 22.5g fat, 12.5g sat fat, 21g total sugars, 0.3g salt

These summer cupcakes are scented with orange flower water and topped with a creamy mascarpone frosting.

INGREDIENTS

1 stick salted butter, softened, or ½ cup soft margarine

½ cup superfine sugar

2 teaspoons orange flower water

2 extra-large eggs, beaten

½ cup almond meal (ground almonds)

1 cup all-purpose flour

1½ teaspoons baking powder

2 tablespoons milk

2½ cups mixed berries, fresh mint leaves, egg white, and sugar, to decorate

frosting

1¼ cups mascarpone cheese

⅓ cup superfine sugar

¼ cup orange juice

1. Preheat the oven to 350°F. Place 12 muffin cups in a muffin pan.

2. Place the butter, superfine sugar, and orange flower water in a large bowl and beat together until light and fluffy. Gradually beat in the eggs. Stir in the almond meal. Sift in the flour and baking powder and, using a metal spoon, fold in gently with the milk.

3. Divide the batter evenly among the muffin cups. Bake in the preheated oven for 15–20 minutes, or until risen, golden and firm to the touch. Transfer to a wire rack and let cool.

4. To make the frosting, put the mascarpone, superfine sugar, and orange juice in a bowl and beat together until smooth.

5. Swirl the frosting over the top of the cupcakes. Brush the berries and mint leaves with egg white, then roll in the sugar to coat. Decorate the cupcakes with the frosted berries and leaves.

2

5

5

COOK'S NOTE
Choose small berries,
such as blueberries
and raspberries, or
hull and halve or
quarter strawberries.

Hummingbird Cupcakes

 MAKES 12

 PREP TIME
25 minutes

 COOKING TIME
15–20 minutes

nutritional information
per cupcake

150 cal, 20g fat, 8g sat fat, 36g total sugars, 0.4g salt

*These delicious cupcakes are packed with pineapple,
banana, and pecans and lightly spiced with cinnamon.
Decorated with a rich and creamy cream cheese frosting,
they are as sweet as nectar!*

INGREDIENTS

1¼ cups all-purpose flour
¾ teaspoon baking soda
1 teaspoon ground cinnamon
½ cup firmly packed
light brown sugar
2 eggs, beaten
½ cup sunflower oil
1 ripe banana, mashed
2 canned pineapple slices,
drained and finely chopped
¼ cup finely chopped pecans,
plus extra sliced pecans
to decorate

frosting
⅔ cup cream cheese
5 tablespoons unsalted butter,
softened
1 teaspoon vanilla extract
2¼ cups confectioners' sugar,
sifted

1. Preheat the oven to 350°F. Place 12 muffin cups in a muffin pan.

2. Sift the flour, baking soda, and cinnamon into a bowl and stir in the sugar. Add the eggs, oil, banana, pineapple, and chopped pecans and mix thoroughly. Divide the batter evenly among the muffin cups.

3. Bake the cupcakes in the preheated oven for 15–20 minutes, or until risen, golden, and firm to the touch. Transfer to a wire rack and let cool.

4. To make the frosting, put the cream cheese, butter, and vanilla extract in a bowl and blend together with a spatula. Beat in the confectioners' sugar until smooth and creamy. Pipe or swirl the frosting on the top of the cupcakes. Decorate with sliced pecans.

Chocolate & Orange Muffins

 MAKES 12

 PREP TIME:
20 minutes
plus cooling

 COOKING TIME:
20 minutes

nutritional information per muffin	408 cal, 21g fat, 9.5g sat fat, 37g total sugars, 0.8g salt

These sweet and crumbly muffins are full of chocolate chips and flavored with tangy orange zest and juice. To make them even more delicious, they have a rich chocolate buttercream topping.

INGREDIENTS

2 oranges
about ½ cup milk
1¾ cups all-purpose flour
⅔ cup unsweetened cocoa powder
1 tablespoon baking powder
pinch of salt
½ cup firmly packed light brown sugar
1 cup semisweet chocolate chips
2 eggs
⅓ cup sunflower oil or 6 tablespoons salted butter, melted and cooled
strips of orange zest, to decorate

frosting
2 ounces semisweet chocolate, broken into pieces
2 tablespoons unsalted butter
2 tablespoons water
1⅓ cups confectioners' sugar

1. Preheat the oven to 400°F. Place 12 muffin cups in a muffin pan.

2. Finely grate the rind from the oranges and squeeze the juice. Add enough milk to make up the juice to 1 cup, then add the orange rind. Sift together the flour, cocoa, baking powder, and salt into a large bowl. Stir in the brown sugar and chocolate chips. Place the eggs in a bowl and beat lightly, then beat in the milk-and-orange mixture and the oil. Make a well in the center of the dry ingredients and pour in the liquid ingredients. Stir gently until just combined; do not overmix. Divide the batter evenly among the muffin cups.

3. Bake in the preheated oven for 20 minutes, or until well risen and firm to the touch. Let cool in the pan for 5 minutes, then transfer to a wire rack to cool completely.

4. To make the frosting, place the chocolate in a heatproof bowl, add the butter and water, then set the bowl over a saucepan of gently simmering water and heat, stirring, until melted. Remove from the heat and sift in the confectioners' sugar. Beat until smooth, then spread the frosting on top of the muffins and decorate with strips of orange zest.

Apple & Cinnamon Muffins

 MAKES 12   PREP TIME: 20 minutes  COOKING TIME: 20–25 minutes

nutritional information per muffin	210 cal, 9g fat, 2g sat fat, 13g total sugars, 0.3g salt

Wholesome muffins made with oats, brown sugar, and grated apple—delicious warm from the oven.

INGREDIENTS

1⅔ cups whole-wheat all-purpose flour

¾ cup rolled oats

2 teaspoons baking powder

1 teaspoon ground cinnamon

½ cup firmly packed light brown sugar

2 extra-large eggs

1 cup low-fat milk

½ cup sunflower oil

1 teaspoon vanilla extract

1 large apple, such as Pippin, peeled, cored, and grated

1. Preheat the oven to 350°F. Place 12 muffin cups in a muffin pan.

2. Sift together the flour, oats, baking powder, and cinnamon into a large bowl, adding any husks that remain in the sifter or strainer. Stir in the sugar.

3. Lightly beat the eggs in a bowl, then beat in the milk, oil, and vanilla extract. Make a well in the center of the dry ingredients and pour in the liquid ingredients. Stir gently until just combined; do not overmix. Stir in the apple.

4. Divide the batter evenly among the muffin cups. Bake in the preheated oven for 20–25 minutes, or until well risen, golden brown, and firm to the touch.

5. Let the muffins cool in the pan for 5 minutes, then serve warm or transfer to a wire rack and let cool.

2

3

3

Tiramisu Cupcakes

 MAKES 12

 PREP TIME:
25 minutes
plus cooling

 COOKING TIME:
15–20 minutes

nutritional information
per cupcake | 284 cal, 18g fat, 11g sat fat, 21g total sugars, 0.2g salt

These scrumptious cupcakes are like the classic Italian dessert—coffee, creamy mascarpone, and Marsala wine.

INGREDIENTS

1 stick unsalted butter, softened
½ cup firmly packed light brown sugar
2 eggs, beaten
1 cup all-purpose flour, sifted
2 teaspoons baking powder
2 teaspoons coffee granules
3 tablespoons confectioners' sugar
¼ cup water
2 tablespoons grated semisweet chocolate, for dusting

frosting
1 cup mascarpone cheese
⅓ cup superfine sugar
2 tablespoons Marsala wine or sweet sherry

1. Preheat the oven to 350°F. Place 12 muffin cups in a muffin pan.

2. Place the butter, brown sugar, eggs, flour, and baking powder in a bowl and beat together until pale and creamy. Divide the batter evenly among the muffin cups.

3. Bake the cupcakes in the preheated oven for 15–20 minutes, or until risen, golden, and firm to the touch.

4. Place the coffee granules, confectioners' sugar, and water in a saucepan and heat gently, stirring, until the coffee and sugar have dissolved. Boil for 1 minute, then let cool for 10 minutes. Brush the coffee syrup over the top of the warm cupcakes. Transfer the cupcakes to a wire rack and let cool.

5. For the frosting, put the mascarpone, sugar, and Marsala in a bowl and beat together until smooth. Spread over the top of the cakes. Using a star template, sprinkle the grated chocolate over the frosting.

2

4

5

BE PREPARED
The flavor of the
cupcakes will improve
if they are made
a day in advance.
Decorate just before
serving.

Blueberry Muffins

 MAKES 12   PREP TIME: 20 minutes   COOKING TIME: 20 minutes

nutritional information per muffin	200 cal, 8g fat, 1.5g sat fat, 12g total sugars, 0.5g salt

Dotted with juicy blueberries and flavored with lemon and vanilla, these buttery muffins will be snapped up as soon as they come out of the oven.

INGREDIENTS

2¼ cups all-purpose flour

1 tablespoon baking powder

pinch of salt

½ cup firmly packed light brown sugar

1 cup frozen blueberries

2 eggs

1 cup whole milk

6 tablespoons salted butter, melted and cooled

1 teaspoon vanilla extract

finely grated rind of 1 lemon

1. Preheat the oven to 400°F. Place 12 muffin cups in a muffin pan. Sift together the flour, baking powder, and salt into a large bowl. Stir in the sugar and blueberries.

2. Lightly beat the eggs in a bowl, then beat in the milk, melted butter, vanilla extract, and lemon rind. Make a well in the center of the dry ingredients and pour in the liquid ingredients. Stir gently until just combined; do not overmix.

3. Divide the batter evenly among the muffin cups. Bake in the preheated oven for about 20 minutes, or until well risen, golden brown, and firm to the touch.

4. Let the muffins cool in the pan for 5 minutes, then serve warm or transfer to a wire rack and let cool.

1

2

3

Candy Cupcakes

 MAKES 12   PREP TIME: 25 minutes plus cooling    COOKING TIME: 18–22 minutes

nutritional information per cupcake	435 cal, 24g fat, 15g sat fat, 42g total sugars, 0.4g salt

These fun cupcakes will make a great treat for children's birthday parties. Why not let them try decorating the cakes themselves? Just make sure you have plenty of candies!

INGREDIENTS

1¼ sticks salted butter, softened, or ⅔ cup soft margarine
¾ cup superfine sugar
3 eggs, beaten
1¾ cups all-purpose flour
1¼ teaspoons baking powder
4 teaspoons strawberry-flavored popping candy
candies of your choice, to decorate (optional)

buttercream
1½ sticks unsalted butter, softened
2 tablespoons whole milk
2¾ cups confectioners' sugar
pink and yellow food coloring

1. Preheat the oven to 350°F. Place 12 muffin cups in a muffin pan.

2. Place the butter and superfine sugar in a large bowl and beat together until pale and creamy. Gradually beat in the eggs. Sift in the flour and baking powder and, using a metal spoon, fold in gently. Fold in half of the popping candy.

3. Divide the batter evenly among the muffin cups. Bake in the preheated oven for 18–22 minutes, or until risen, golden, and firm to the touch. Transfer to a wire rack and let cool.

4. To make the buttercream, place the butter in a bowl and beat until pale and creamy. Beat in the milk, then gradually sift in the confectioners' sugar and continue beating for 2–3 minutes, or until the buttercream is light and fluffy. Divide the buttercream between two bowls and beat a little pink or yellow food coloring into each bowl.

5. Pipe or swirl the buttercream on top of the cupcakes and decorate with candies, if using. Sprinkle over the remaining popping candy just before serving.

Fudge Nut Muffins

 MAKES 12   PREP TIME 20 minutes   COOKING TIME 20–25 minutes

nutritional information per muffin	280 cal, 13g fat, 5g sat fat, 18g total sugars, 0.6g salt

Peanut butter gives these muffins a wonderful nutty flavor and a beautiful crunchy texture.

INGREDIENTS

2 cups all-purpose flour

4 teaspoons baking powder

⅓ cup superfine sugar

⅓ cup chunky peanut butter

1 extra-large egg

¾ cup whole milk

4 tablespoons salted butter, melted and cooled

5½ ounces vanilla fudge, cut into small pieces

3 tablespoons coarsely chopped unsalted peanuts

1. Preheat the oven to 400°F. Place 12 muffin cups in a muffin pan. Sift together the flour and baking powder into a large bowl. Stir in the sugar. Add the peanut butter and stir until the mixture resembles bread crumbs.

2. Lightly beat the egg in a bowl, then beat in the milk and melted butter. Make a well in the center of the dry ingredients, pour in the liquid ingredients, and add the fudge pieces. Stir gently until just combined; do not overmix.

3. Divide the batter evenly among the muffin cups. Sprinkle the peanuts over the tops of the muffins. Bake in the preheated oven for 20–25 minutes, or until well risen, golden brown, and firm to the touch.

4. Let the muffins cool in the pan for 5 minutes, then serve warm or transfer to a wire rack and let cool.

2

2

4

Apple Streusel Cupcakes

 MAKES 14   PREP TIME: 25 minutes   COOKING TIME: 20 minutes

nutritional information per cupcake	160 cal, 6g fat, 3.5g sat fat, 13g total sugars, 0.3g salt

Topped with a spiced crumb, these fruity cupcakes make a great dessert served warm with whipped cream.

INGREDIENTS

½ teaspoon baking soda
1 cup applesauce (from a jar)
½ stick salted butter, softened
½ cup raw brown sugar
1 extra-large egg, beaten
1⅓ cups all-purpose flour
2 teaspoons baking powder
½ teaspoon ground cinnamon
½ teaspoon freshly grated nutmeg

topping
⅓ cup all-purpose flour
¼ cup raw brown sugar
¼ teaspoon ground cinnamon
¼ teaspoon freshly grated nutmeg
2½ tablespoons unsalted butter, softened

1. Preheat the oven to 350°F. Place 14 muffin cups in two muffin pans.

2. To make the topping, put the flour, raw brown sugar, cinnamon, and nutmeg in a bowl. Cut the butter into small pieces, then add to the bowl and rub it in with your fingertips until the mixture resembles fine bread crumbs.

3. Add the baking soda to the applesauce and stir until dissolved. Place the butter and raw brown sugar in a large bowl and beat together until pale and creamy. Gradually beat in the egg. Sift in the flour, baking powder, cinnamon, and nutmeg and, using a metal spoon, fold into the mixture, alternating with the applesauce mixture.

4. Divide the batter evenly among the muffin cups. Sprinkle the topping over the cupcakes and press down gently. Bake in the preheated oven for 20 minutes, or until risen, golden, and firm to the touch. Transfer to a wire rack and let cool.

2

3

3

FREEZING TIP
Freeze for up to two
months packed into a
freezer-proof container.
Let thaw at room
temperature for
2-3 hours.

Chocolate Chip Cookies *68*

Double Chocolate Pecan Blondies *70*

Vanilla Macarons *72*

Cinnamon Stars *74*

Raisin Oat Bars *76*

Sugar Cookies *78*

Double Chocolate Whoopie Pies *80*

Classic Oatmeal Cookies *82*

Butterscotch Cookies *84*

Chocolate & Cinnamon Brownies *86*

Peanut Butter Cookies *88*

Apricot Oat Bars *90*

Salted Caramel Squares *92*

Marshmallow S'mores *94*

Cookies & Bars

Chocolate Chip Cookies

 MAKES 8   PREP TIME: 10 minutes   COOKING TIME: 10–12 minutes

nutritional information per cookie | 353 cal, 19g fat, 6g sat fat, 27g total sugars, 0.5g salt

These traditional chocolate-laden cookies are crisp on the outside and chewy in the middle. Delicious warm from the oven, they also keep well stored in an airtight container.

INGREDIENTS

unsalted butter, melted, for greasing
1⅓ cups all-purpose flour, sifted
1 teaspoon baking powder
1 stick margarine, melted
⅓ cup firmly packed light brown sugar
¼ cup superfine sugar
½ teaspoon vanilla extract
1 egg, beaten
¾ cup semisweet chocolate chips

1. Preheat the oven to 375°F. Lightly grease two baking sheets.

2. Place all of the ingredients in a large mixing bowl and beat until well combined.

3. Place tablespoons of the dough on the prepared baking sheets, spaced well apart.

4. Bake in the preheated oven for 10–12 minutes, or until golden brown. Transfer to a wire rack and let cool.

1

2

3

SOMETHING DIFFERENT
Add some coarsely chopped nuts to the cookie dough—try pecans, hazelnuts, or blanched almonds.

Double Chocolate Pecan Blondies

 MAKES 12

 PREP TIME:
30 minutes
plus cooling

 COOKING TIME:
35–40 minutes

nutritional information per cake	346 cal, 21g fat, 9g sat fat, 28g total sugars, 0.25g salt

With chunks of white and dark chocolate and crunchy pecans, these tempting bars are an indulgent treat.

INGREDIENTS

9 ounces white chocolate, broken into pieces

3 tablespoons salted butter, plus extra for greasing

6 ounces semisweet chocolate

2 extra-large eggs, beaten

⅓ cup superfine sugar

1 cup all-purpose flour

1½ teaspoons baking powder

1 cup coarsely chopped pecans

1. Preheat the oven to 350°F. Grease a shallow 8-inch square baking pan.

2. Place 3 ounces of the white chocolate in a heatproof bowl and add the butter. Set the bowl over a saucepan of gently simmering water and heat, stirring occasionally, until melted and smooth. Meanwhile, coarsely chop the remaining white and semisweet chocolate.

3. Beat together the eggs and sugar in a large bowl, then stir in the melted chocolate mixture. Sift the flour and baking powder over the mixture. Add the chopped chocolate and pecans. Mix well.

4. Spoon the batter into the prepared pan and smooth the surface. Bake in the preheated oven for 35–40 minutes, or until golden brown and just firm to the touch in the center. Let stand in the pan until completely cooled and the chocolate chunks inside have set, then invert and cut into pieces.

2

3

4

COOK'S NOTE
Be careful to avoid overcooking the blondies or you'll lose that wonderful soft texture.

Vanilla Macarons

 MAKES 16

 PREP TIME: 20 minutes plus cooling

 COOKING TIME: 10–15 minutes

nutritional information per cake	125 cal, 5.5g fat, 2g sat fat, 17.5g total sugars, trace salt

Originating from France, these melt-in-the-mouth petits fours are made with almond meal, sugar, and egg whites.

INGREDIENTS

¾ cup almond meal (ground almonds)

1 cup confectioners' sugar

2 extra-large egg whites

¼ cup superfine sugar

½ teaspoon vanilla extract

filling

4 tablespoons unsalted butter, softened

½ teaspoon vanilla extract

1 cup confectioners' sugar, sifted

1. Line two baking sheets with parchment paper. Place the almond meal and confectioners' sugar in a food processor and process for 15 seconds. Sift the mixture into a bowl.

2. Place the egg whites into a clean, grease-free bowl and beat until holding soft peaks. Gradually beat in the superfine sugar to make a firm, glossy meringue. Beat in the vanilla extract.

3. Using a spatula, fold the almond mixture into the meringue one-third at a time. When all the dry ingredients are thoroughly incorporated, continue to cut and fold the mixture until it forms a shiny batter with a thick, ribbonlike consistency.

4. Pour the batter into a pastry bag fitted with a ½-inch plain tip. Pipe 32 small mounds onto the prepared baking sheets. Tap the baking sheets firmly onto a surface to remove air bubbles. Let stand at room temperature for 30 minutes. Preheat the oven to 325°F.

5. Bake in the preheated oven for 10–15 minutes. Cool for 10 minutes, then carefully peel the macarons off the parchment paper. Let cool completely.

6. To make the filling, beat the butter and vanilla extract in a bowl until pale and fluffy. Gradually beat in the confectioners' sugar until smooth and creamy. Use to sandwich pairs of macarons together.

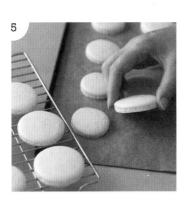

Cinnamon Stars

 MAKES 20   PREP TIME: 25 minutes plus chilling   COOKING TIME: 25 minutes

nutritional information per cookie	116 cal, 8g fat, 0.6g sat fat, 9g total sugars, trace salt

These beautiful little spiced hazelnut star cookies are perfect to give as a homemade Christmas gift.

INGREDIENTS

2 egg whites

1⅓ cups confectioners' sugar, plus extra for dusting

3 cups ground hazelnuts, roasted

1 tablespoon ground cinnamon

1. Beat the egg whites in a clean, grease-free bowl until stiff. Stir in the sugar until thoroughly combined, then continue to beat until thick and glossy.

2. Remove ¼ cup of this mixture and set aside. Then fold the hazelnuts and cinnamon into the remaining mixture to make a stiff dough. Chill in the refrigerator for about an hour.

3. Preheat the oven to 275°F. Line two baking sheets with parchment paper. Roll out the dough to ½ inch thick on a surface amply dusted with confectioners' sugar.

4. Cut the dough into shapes, using a 2-inch star-shape cutter, dusting with confectioners' sugar to prevent the dough from sticking. Reroll as necessary until all of the mixture is used.

5. Place the cookies on the prepared baking sheets, spaced well apart, and spread the top of each star with the reserved egg white icing.

6. Bake in the preheated oven for 25 minutes, or until the cookies are still white and crisp on top but slightly soft and moist underneath. Turn off the oven and open the oven door to release the heat and dry the cookies out in the oven for 10 more minutes. Transfer to wire racks to cool completely.

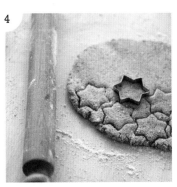

Raisin Oat Bars

 MAKES 14

 PREP TIME:
15 minutes

 COOKING TIME:
15–20 minutes

nutritional information
per bar | 147 cal, 8g fat, 5g sat fat, 12g total sugars, 0.15g salt

These simple oat bars have a sweet buttery flavor and are studded with juicy raisins. You can replace the raisins with golden raisins or dried currants or try milk or semisweet chocolate chips instead.

INGREDIENTS

1½ cups rolled oats
½ cup raw brown sugar
½ cup raisins
1 stick salted butter, melted,
plus extra for greasing

1. Preheat the oven to 375°F. Grease a shallow 11 x 7-inch baking pan.

2. Combine the oats, sugar, and raisins with the butter in a mixing bowl, stirring well. Spoon the mixture into the prepared pan and press down firmly with the back of a spoon. Bake in the preheated oven for 15–20 minutes, or until golden.

3. Using a sharp knife, mark into 14 bars, then let cool in the pan for 10 minutes. Carefully transfer the bars to a wire rack to cool completely.

2

2

3

HEALTHY HINT
Cut the oat bars into smaller pieces for a less calorific sweet treat.

Sugar Cookies

 MAKES 20

 PREP TIME:
20 minutes
plus chilling

 COOKING TIME
10–12 minutes

nutritional information
per cookie　　90 cal, 5g fat, 3g sat fat, 3g total sugars, trace salt

Crisp, light, and buttery with a hint of lemon and a sweet sugary coating—the perfect cookie!

INGREDIENTS

1 stick salted butter, softened, plus extra for greasing

¼ cup superfine sugar, plus extra for sprinkling

1 teaspoon finely grated lemon rind

1 egg yolk

1⅓ cups all-purpose flour, plus extra for dusting

1. Place the butter and sugar in a bowl and beat together until pale and creamy. Beat in the lemon rind and egg yolk. Sift in the flour and mix to a soft dough. Turn out onto a floured surface and knead until smooth, adding a little more flour, if necessary. Halve the dough, shape into balls, wrap in plastic wrap, and chill in the refrigerator for 1 hour.

2. Preheat the oven to 350°F. Lightly grease two large baking sheets.

3. Roll out the dough on a lightly floured surface to a thickness of ¼ inch. Using 2¾-inch flower-shape and heart-shape cutters, stamp out 20 cookies, rerolling the dough as necessary. Place on the prepared baking sheets and sprinkle with sugar.

4. Bake in the preheated oven for 10–12 minutes, or until pale golden. Let cool on the baking sheets for 2–3 minutes, then transfer to a wire rack to cool completely.

1
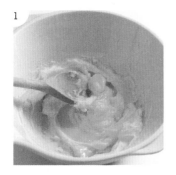

3

3

Double Chocolate Whoopie Pies

 MAKES 12

 PREP TIME:
30 minutes
plus chilling

 COOKING TIME:
20–25 minutes

nutritional information per cake	
480 cal, 35g fat, 19g sat fat, 26g total sugars, 0.8g salt	

What could be more delicious than two little cakes sandwiched together with a creamy filling? This double chocolate version is simply irresistible.

INGREDIENTS

1⅔ cups all-purpose flour

1½ teaspoons baking soda

¼ cup unsweetened cocoa powder

large pinch of salt

6 tablespoons salted butter, softened

⅓ cup vegetable shortening

⅔ cup firmly packed, light brown sugar

1 ounce semisweet chocolate, finely grated

1 extra-large egg, beaten

½ cup whole milk

¼ cup semisweet chocolate strands

white chocolate filling

6 ounces white chocolate, broken into pieces

2 tablespoons milk

1¼ cups heavy cream

1. Preheat the oven to 350°F. Line two to three large baking sheets with parchment paper. Sift together the all-purpose flour, baking soda, cocoa powder, and salt.

2. Place the butter, vegetable shortening, sugar, and grated chocolate in a large bowl and beat with an electric handheld mixer until pale and fluffy. Beat in the egg, followed by half the flour mixture, then the milk. Stir in the rest of the flour mixture and mix until thoroughly incorporated.

3. Pipe or spoon 24 mounds of the batter onto the prepared baking sheets, spaced well apart to allow for spreading. Bake in the preheated oven, one sheet at a time, for 10–12 minutes, or until risen and just firm to the touch. Cool for 5 minutes, then, using a spatula, transfer to a wire rack and let cool completely.

4. For the filling, place the chocolate and milk in a heatproof bowl set over a saucepan of simmering water. Heat until the chocolate has melted, stirring occasionally. Remove from the heat and let cool for 30 minutes. Using an electric mixer, whip the cream until holding firm peaks. Fold in the chocolate. Cover and chill in the refrigerator for 30–45 minutes, or until firm enough to spread.

5. To assemble, spread or pipe the chocolate filling on the flat side of half of the cakes. Top with the rest of the cakes. Spread the chocolate strands on a plate and gently roll the edges of each whoopie pie in the strands to lightly coat.

Classic Oatmeal Cookies

 MAKES 30   PREP TIME: 15 minutes   COOKING TIME 15 minutes

nutritional information per cookie	141 cal, 6g fat, 3g sat fat, 9g total sugars, 0.3g salt

These simple cookies are made from pantry ingredients and take minutes to make and bake.

INGREDIENTS

1½ sticks salted butter, softened, plus extra for greasing
1⅓ cups raw brown sugar
1 egg, beaten
¼ cup water
1 teaspoon vanilla extract
4 cups rolled oats
1 cup all-purpose flour
1 teaspoon salt
½ teaspoon baking soda

1. Preheat the oven to 350°F. Grease two large baking sheets.

2. Place the butter and sugar in a large bowl and beat together until pale and creamy. Beat in the egg, water, and vanilla extract until the mixture is smooth. Mix together the oats, flour, salt, and baking soda in a separate bowl, then gradually stir the oat mixture into the creamed mixture until thoroughly combined.

3. Place tablespoonfuls of the dough on the prepared baking sheets, spaced well apart.

4. Bake in the preheated oven for 15 minutes, or until golden brown. Transfer to a wire rack to cool completely.

2

2

3

Butterscotch Cookies

nutritional information per cookie   118 cal, 5.5g fat, 3g sat fat, 9.5g total sugars, 0.35g salt

Chunks of melted toffee give these golden brown cookies a deliciously chewy texture.

INGREDIENTS

¾ cup firmly packed light brown sugar
1 stick salted butter, softened
1 extra-large egg, beaten
1 teaspoon vanilla extract
1⅔ cups all-purpose flour
1 teaspoon baking soda
2¼ teaspoons baking powder
10 toffees, chopped

1. Preheat the oven to 350°F. Line three large baking sheets with parchment paper.

2. Put the sugar and butter into a bowl and beat together until creamy. Beat in the egg and vanilla extract. Sift together the flour, baking soda, and baking powder and stir in thoroughly. Stir in the toffees.

3. Place walnut-size spoonfuls of the dough on the prepared baking sheets, spaced well apart.

4. Bake in the preheated oven for 8–10 minutes, or until light golden brown. Let cool on the baking sheets, then peel away from the parchment paper.

2

3
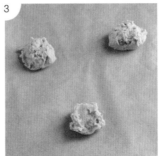

4

COOK'S NOTE
Let the toffees stand in a warm place for about 30 minutes before chopping so they soften up a little.

Chocolate & Cinnamon Brownies

 MAKES 16

 PREP TIME: 40 minutes plus cooling

 COOKING TIME: 35–40 minutes

nutritional information per brownie	348 cal, 19g fat, 9g sat fat, 29g total sugars, 0.3g salt

An all-time favorite, chocolate brownies are really easy to make, keep well, and always taste fantastic. This version is full of pecans, lightly spiced with ground cinnamon, and topped with a sweet white chocolate frosting.

INGREDIENTS

4 ounces semisweet chocolate, broken into pieces

1¾ sticks salted butter, plus extra for greasing

1 cup pecan halves

1¼ cups superfine sugar

4 eggs, beaten

1¾ cups all-purpose flour

2 teaspoons ground cinnamon

2 ounces white chocolate, broken into pieces

2 tablespoons milk

1 cup confectioners' sugar

1. Preheat the oven to 350°F. Grease a shallow 9-inch square cake pan.

2. Melt the semisweet chocolate and 1½ sticks of the butter in a heatproof bowl set over a saucepan of gently simmering water. Remove from the heat and let cool slightly.

3. Set 16 pecan halves to one side for decoration and chop the rest. Beat together the superfine sugar and eggs with an electric mixer until thick and creamy. Then fold in the chocolate mixture, flour, cinnamon, and chopped pecans.

4. Transfer the batter to the prepared pan and bake in the preheated oven for 35–40 minutes, or until just firm to the touch. Let cool in the pan.

5. Melt the remaining butter and white chocolate in a heatproof bowl set over a saucepan of gently simmering water. Remove from the heat and beat in the milk and confectioners' sugar. Spread this mixture over the cooled brownies. Let set for 30 minutes, then cut into 16 squares and top each square with a pecan half.

Peanut Butter Cookies

 MAKES 15

 PREP TIME:
20 minutes
plus chilling

 COOKING TIME
15 minutes

nutritional information
per cookie | 260 cal, 15g fat, 6g sat fat, 16g total sugars, 0.5g salt

Rich and buttery with a lovely peanut flavor, these simple cookies taste great with a glass of cold milk.

INGREDIENTS

1⅓ cups all-purpose flour
½ teaspoon baking powder
½ teaspoon salt
1 cup smooth peanut butter
1 stick salted butter, softened
1¼ teaspoons vanilla extract
½ cup firmly packed
light brown sugar
½ cup superfine sugar
2 eggs

1. Sift together the flour, baking powder, and salt into a bowl and set aside. Beat together the peanut butter, butter, and vanilla extract until smooth in another bowl. Beat in the brown sugar and superfine sugar for 1 minute, then beat in the eggs one at a time. Stir in the flour mixture in two batches.

2. Halve the dough, shape into balls, wrap in plastic wrap, and chill in the refrigerator for at least 2 hours. Meanwhile, preheat the oven to 350°F. Line two baking sheets with parchment paper or leave uncovered and ungreased.

3. Roll or scoop the dough into 1½-inch balls and place them on the prepared baking sheets, spaced well apart. Use a fork to flatten each ball by making a crisscross pattern. Bake in the preheated oven for 15 minutes, or until golden. Remove the cookies from the oven and let cool on the baking sheet for 5 minutes. Using a spatula, transfer to a wire rack to cool completely.

1

2

3

BE PREPARED
The wrapped cookie dough can be kept in the refrigerator for 2-3 days before baking.

Apricot Oat Bars

MAKES 10
PREP TIME: 15 minutes
COOKING TIME: 20–25 minutes

nutritional information per bar	296 cal, 17g fat, 3.5g sat fat, 18g total sugars, 0.3g salt

Oat bars are really easy to make and taste so much better than store-bought cakes. Great for lunch bags or fiber-packed snacks, this version is flavored with apricots, honey, and sesame seeds.

INGREDIENTS

1½ sticks margarine, plus extra for greasing
⅓ cup raw brown sugar
¼ cup honey
1 cup chopped dried apricots
2 teaspoons sesame seeds
2½ cups rolled oats

1. Preheat the oven to 350°F. Grease a shallow 10½ x 6½-inch baking pan.

2. Put the margarine, sugar, and honey into a small saucepan over low heat and heat until the ingredients have melted together—do not boil. When the ingredients are well combined, stir in the apricots, sesame seeds, and oats.

3. Spoon the mixture into the prepared pan and smooth the surface with the back of a spoon. Bake in the preheated oven for 20–25 minutes, or until golden brown.

4. Remove from the oven, cut into 10 bars, and let cool completely before removing from the pan.

2

2

3

COOK'S NOTE
Oat bars are still
soft when they
come out of the oven—
they set on cooling.

Salted Caramel Squares

 MAKES 16   PREP TIME
30 minutes
plus chilling   COOKING TIME
15 minutes

nutritional information per square	356 cal, 21g fat, 12g sat fat, 29g total sugars, 0.5g salt

A touch of sea salt added to the caramel gives this sweet treat a modern twist.

INGREDIENTS

1 stick salted butter, softened, plus extra for greasing
¼ cup superfine sugar
1⅓ cups all-purpose flour
½ cup almond meal (ground almonds)

topping
1½ sticks salted butter
½ cup superfine sugar
3 tablespoons corn syrup
1 (14-ounce) can condensed milk
¼ teaspoon sea salt crystals
3 ounces semisweet chocolate, melted

1. Preheat the oven to 350°F. Grease a shallow 8-inch square cake pan.

2. Put the butter and sugar into a bowl and beat together until pale and creamy. Sift in the flour and add the almond meal. Use clean hands to mix and knead to a crumbly dough. Press into the bottom of the prepared pan and prick the surface all over with a fork. Bake in the preheated oven for 15 minutes, or until pale golden. Let cool.

3. To make the topping, put the butter, sugar, corn syrup, and condensed milk into a heavy saucepan over low heat and heat gently until the sugar has dissolved. Increase the heat to medium, bring to a boil, then simmer for 6–8 minutes, stirring continuously, until the mixture becomes thick. Stir in half the salt, then quickly pour the caramel over the shortbread crust. Sprinkle over the remaining salt.

4. Spoon the chocolate into a paper pastry bag and snip off the end. Pipe the chocolate over the caramel and swirl with the tip of a knife. Let cool, then chill for 2 hours, or until firm. Cut into 16 squares.

2

3

4

A heavy saucepan is essential for making the caramel and you must stir the mixture continuously to prevent it from burning.

Marshmallow S'mores

 MAKES 15

 PREP TIME:
30 minutes
plus chilling

 COOKING TIME:
12–17 minutes

nutritional information
per cookie | 371 cal, 20g fat, 12g sat fat, 30g total sugars, 0.4g salt

The name s'mores is a shortened version of "some more"—and everyone will want more of these chocolate cookies with a marshmallow filling!

INGREDIENTS

2 sticks salted butter, softened

⅔ cup superfine sugar

2 teaspoons finely grated orange rind

1 egg yolk, lightly beaten

2 cups all-purpose flour

¼ cup unsweetened cocoa powder

½ teaspoon ground cinnamon

pinch of salt

30 yellow marshmallows, halved horizontally

10 ounces semisweet chocolate, broken into pieces

¼ cup orange marmalade

15 walnut halves, to decorate

1. Place the butter, sugar, and orange rind in a large bowl and beat together until light and fluffy, then beat in the egg yolk. Sift together the flour, cocoa, cinnamon, and salt into the mixture and stir until combined. Halve the dough, shape into balls, wrap in plastic wrap, and chill in the refrigerator for 30–60 minutes.

2. Preheat the oven to 375°F. Line several large baking sheets with parchment paper. Unwrap the dough and roll out between two sheets of parchment paper. Cut out 30 cookies with a 2½-inch fluted round cutter and place them on the prepared baking sheets, spaced well apart. Bake in the preheated oven for 10–15 minutes. Let cool for 5 minutes. Turn half of the cookies upside down and put four marshmallow halves on each of the turned-over cookies. Bake these marshmallow-topped cookies for an additional 1–2 minutes. Let all the cookies cool on wire racks for 30 minutes.

3. Place the chocolate in a heatproof bowl, set the bowl over a saucepan of gently simmering water, and heat until melted. Line a baking sheet with parchment paper. Spread the marmalade over the undersides of the uncovered cookies and place them on top of the marshmallow-covered cookies. Dip the cookies in the melted chocolate to coat. Place a walnut half in the center of each cookie and let set.

Pies, Pastries & Breads

Apple Pie

 SERVES 6

 PREP TIME:
40 minutes
plus chilling

 COOKING TIME:
50 minutes

nutritional information per serving	567 cal, 28g fat, 13.5g sat fat, 32g total sugars, 0.5g salt

A golden pie crust filled to the brim with apples, sugar, and a hint of cinnamon—this is the ultimate apple pie!

INGREDIENTS

pie dough
2¾ cups all-purpose flour, plus extra for dusting

pinch of salt

6 tablespoons salted butter or margarine, diced

⅓ cup plus 1 tablespoon lard or vegetable shortening, diced

6 tablespoons cold water

beaten egg or milk, for glazing

filling
3–4 large cooking apples (about 1¾–2¼ pounds), such as Granny Smith, Golden Delicious, or Pippin, peeled, cored, and sliced

⅔ cup superfine sugar, plus extra for sprinkling

½–1 teaspoon ground cinnamon, apple pie spice, or ground ginger

1. To make the pie dough, sift the flour and salt into a mixing bowl. Add the butter and lard and rub in with your fingertips until the mixture resembles fine bread crumbs. Add the water and gather the mixture together into a dough. Wrap the dough in plastic wrap and chill in the refrigerator for 30 minutes.

2. Preheat the oven to 425°F. Roll out almost two-thirds of the dough thinly on a lightly floured surface and use to line a deep 9-inch pie plate.

3. To make the filling, place the apple slices, sugar, and spice in a bowl and mix together thoroughly. Pack the apple mixture into the pie shell; the filling can come up above the rim. Add 1–2 tablespoons of water, if needed, particularly if the apples are not juicy.

4. Roll out the remaining dough on a lightly floured surface to form a lid. Dampen the edges of the pie rim with water and position the lid, pressing the edges firmly together. Trim and crimp the edges. Use the trimmings to cut out leaves or other shapes to decorate the top of the pie. Dampen and attach. Glaze the top of the pie with beaten egg, make 1–2 slits in the top and place the pie plate on a baking sheet.

5. Bake in the preheated oven for 20 minutes, then reduce the temperature to 350°F and bake for an additional 30 minutes, or until the pastry is a light golden brown. Serve hot or cold, sprinkled with sugar.

Five-Grain Loaf

 MAKES
1 loaf

 PREP TIME:
20 minutes
plus rising

 COOKING TIME:
25–30 minutes

nutritional information per loaf	2,544 cal, 84g fat, 12g sat fat, 24g total sugars, 4.8g salt

Packed full of nutritious seeds and made with whole-wheat flour, this loaf is full of fiber.

INGREDIENTS

2¼ cups whole-wheat bread flour, plus extra for dusting

1⅔ cups white bread flour

1 teaspoon salt

⅔ cup mixed seeds, including sesame, pumpkin, sunflower, hemp, and flaxseed

2¼ teaspoons active dry yeast

1 tablespoon light brown sugar

2 tablespoons sunflower oil, plus extra for greasing

1¼ cups lukewarm water

1. Lightly grease a baking sheet with oil. Mix the whole-wheat flour, white flour, salt, mixed seeds, and yeast in a large bowl. Stir in the sugar. Mix together the oil and water. Make a well in the center of the dry ingredients and pour in the liquid ingredients. Mix with a knife to make a soft, sticky dough.

2. Invert the dough onto a lightly floured surface and knead for 5–7 minutes, or until smooth and elastic. Shape the dough into a round ball and place on the prepared baking sheet. Dust the top of the loaf with whole-wheat flour and let stand in a warm place for 1–1½ hours, or until doubled in size.

3. Meanwhile, preheat the oven to 425°F. Bake the loaf in the preheated oven for 5 minutes. Reduce the oven temperature to 400°F and bake for an additional 20–25 minutes, or until golden brown and the bottom sounds hollow when tapped with your knuckles. Transfer to a wire rack to cool.

1

2

3

SOMETHING
DIFFERENT
To make individual
rolls, divide and
shape the dough
into 12 round balls
and bake for
10-15 minutes
at 400°F.

Key Lime Pie

 SERVES 8

 PREP TIME:
30 minutes
plus chilling

 COOKING TIME:
20 minutes

nutritional information per serving	377 cal, 19g fat, 10g sat fat, 33g total sugars, 0.7g salt

This refreshing sweet lime pie originates from the Florida Keys and is named after the limes that are grown in the area.

INGREDIENTS

crumb crust
25 Graham crackers or gingersnaps (6 ounces)
2 tablespoons superfine sugar
½ teaspoon ground cinnamon
5 tablespoons salted butter, melted, plus extra for greasing

filling
1 (14-ounce) can condensed milk
½ cup freshly squeezed lime juice
finely grated rind of 3 limes
4 egg yolks
whipped cream, to serve

1. Preheat the oven to 325°F. Lightly grease a 9-inch tart pan, about 1½ inches deep. To make the crumb crust, put the cookies, sugar, and cinnamon in a food processor and process until fine crumbs form—do not overprocess to a powder. Add the melted butter and process again until moistened.

2. Transfer the crumb mixture to the prepared tart pan and press over the bottom and up the sides. Place the tart pan on a baking sheet and bake in the preheated oven for 5 minutes. Meanwhile, to make the filling, beat together the condensed milk, lime juice, lime rind, and egg yolks in a bowl until well blended.

3. Remove the tart pan from the oven, pour the filling into the crumb crust, and spread out to the edges. Return to the oven for an additional 15 minutes, or until the filling is set around the edges but still wobbly in the center. Let cool completely on a wire rack, then cover and chill for at least 2 hours. Spread with whipped cream and serve.

1

2

3

SOMETHING DIFFERENT

Instead of cream, top the pie with meringue and brown briefly in a hot oven.

Whole-Wheat Loaf

MAKES
1 loaf

PREP TIME:
20 minutes
plus rising

COOKING TIME:
30 minutes

nutritional information per loaf	1,024 cal, 27g fat, 3g sat fat, 34g total sugars, 5g salt

Made with whole-wheat flour, which contains the whole wheat grain, this loaf will have more flavor, fiber, and nutrients than white bread.

INGREDIENTS

1⅔ cups whole-wheat bread flour, plus extra for dusting

1 tablespoon powdered milk

1 teaspoon salt

2 tablespoons light brown sugar

1 teaspoon active dry yeast

1½ tablespoons sunflower oil, plus extra for greasing

¾ cup lukewarm water

1. Place the flour, powdered milk, salt, sugar, and yeast in a large bowl. Pour in the oil and add the water, then mix well to make a smooth dough.

2. Invert onto a lightly floured surface and knead well for about 10 minutes, or until smooth. Brush a bowl with oil. Shape the dough into a ball, place it in the bowl, and cover with a damp dish towel. Let rise in a warm place for 1 hour, or until the dough has doubled in volume.

3. Preheat the oven to 425°F. Oil a 9-inch loaf pan. Invert the dough onto a lightly floured surface and knead for 1 minute, or until smooth. Shape the dough the length of the pan and three times the width. Fold the dough into three lengthwise and place it in the pan with the seam underneath. Cover and let stand in a warm place for 30 minutes, or until it has risen above the pan.

4. Place in the preheated oven and bake for 30 minutes, or until firm and golden brown. Test that the loaf is cooked by tapping on the base with your knuckles—it should sound hollow. Transfer to a wire rack to cool.

Pumpkin Pie

 SERVES 8   PREP TIME: 25 minutes   COOKING TIME: 1 hour

nutritional information per serving	630 cal, 42g fat, 21g sat fat, 33g total sugars, 0.98g salt

This traditional pie makes a wonderful dessert for Thanksgiving, but it's so good that you can prepare it at other times during the year.

INGREDIENTS

all-purpose flour, for dusting
1 sheet store-bought rolled dough pie crust, thawed, if frozen
1 (15-ounce) can pumpkin puree
2 eggs, lightly beaten
¾ cup sugar
1 teaspoon ground cinnamon
½ teaspoon ground ginger
¼ teaspoon ground cloves
½ teaspoon salt
1 (12-fluid-ounce) can evaporated milk

brandy whipped cream
1½ cups heavy cream
½ cup confectioners' sugar
1 tablespoon brandy, or to taste
1 tablespoon light rum or dark rum, or to taste
freshly grated nutmeg, to decorate

1. Preheat the oven to 400°F. Lightly dust a rolling pin with flour and use to roll out the dough on a lightly floured surface into a 12-inch circle. Line a deep 9-inch pie plate with the pie dough, trimming off the excess. Line the pie dough shell with parchment paper and fill with pie weights or dried beans.

2. Bake in the preheated oven for 10 minutes. Remove from the oven and take out the paper and weights. Reduce the oven temperature to 350°F.

3. Meanwhile, put the pumpkin puree, eggs, sugar, cinnamon, ginger, cloves, and salt into a bowl and beat together, then beat in the evaporated milk. Pour the mixture into the pie dough shell, return to the oven, and bake for 40–50 minutes, until the filling is set and a knife inserted in the center comes out clean. Transfer to a wire rack and set aside to cool completely.

4. While the pie is baking, make the brandy whipped cream. Put the cream in a bowl and beat until it has thickened and increased in volume. Just as it starts to stiffen, sift in the confectioners' sugar and continue beating until it holds stiff peaks. Add the brandy and rum and beat, being careful not to overbeat or the mixture will separate. Cover and chill until required. When ready to serve, grate some nutmeg over the whipped cream. Serve the pie with the cream.

Lemon Meringue Pie

 SERVES 8

 PREP TIME:
40 minutes
plus chilling

 COOKING TIME:
55 minutes

nutritional information per serving	300 cal, 12g fat, 6.5g sat fat, 27g total sugars, 0.25g salt

The beauty of this classic dessert is the way the sweet pastry shell and sugary meringue perfectly complement the deliciously tangy lemon filling.

INGREDIENTS

pie dough
1 cup plus 2 tablespoons all-purpose flour, plus extra for dusting

6 tablespoons salted butter, diced, plus extra for greasing

¼ cup confectioners' sugar, sifted

finely grated rind of ½ lemon

½ egg yolk, beaten

1½ tablespoons milk

filling
3 tablespoons cornstarch

1¼ cups water

juice and grated rind of 2 lemons

1 cup superfine sugar

2 eggs, separated

1. To make the dough, sift the flour into a bowl. Rub in the butter with your fingertips until the mixture resembles fine bread crumbs. Mix in the remaining pastry ingredients to make a dough. Invert onto a lightly floured surface and knead briefly. Wrap in plastic wrap and chill in the refrigerator for 30 minutes.

2. Preheat the oven to 350°F. Grease an 8-inch tart pan. Roll out the dough to a thickness of ¼ inch on a lightly floured surface, then use it to line the bottom and sides of the pan. Prick all over with a fork, line with parchment paper, and fill with pie weights or dried beans. Bake in the preheated oven for 15 minutes. Remove the pastry shell from the oven and take out the paper and weights. Reduce the oven temperature to 300°F.

3. To make the filling, mix the cornstarch with a little of the water to form a paste. Put the remaining water in a saucepan. Stir in the lemon juice, lemon rind, and cornstarch paste. Bring to a boil, stirring. Cook for 2 minutes. Let cool slightly. Stir in ⅓ cup of the superfine sugar and the egg yolks, then pour into the pastry shell.

4. Beat the egg whites in a clean, grease-free bowl until they hold stiff peaks. Gradually beat in the remaining superfine sugar and spread over the pie. Bake for an additional 40 minutes. Remove from the oven, cool, and serve.

3

4

Crusty White Loaf

MAKES	PREP TIME	COOKING TIME
1 loaf	20 minutes plus rising	30 minutes

nutritional information per loaf	2,123 cal, 42g fat, 18g sat fat, 17g total sugars, 7.7g salt

Baking your own bread is a satisfying and rewarding pastime. If you're a novice baker, then start with this simple white loaf.

INGREDIENTS

1 egg
1 egg yolk
⅔–1 cup lukewarm water
3⅔ cups white bread flour, plus extra for dusting
1½ teaspoons salt
2 teaspoons sugar
1 teaspoon active dry yeast
2 tablespoons salted butter, diced
sunflower oil, for greasing

1. Place the egg and egg yolk in a bowl and beat lightly to mix. Add enough lukewarm water to make up to 1¼ cups. Stir well.

2. Place the flour, salt, sugar, and yeast in a large bowl. Add the butter and rub it in with your fingertips until the mixture resembles bread crumbs. Make a well in the center, add the egg mixture, and work to a smooth dough.

3. Invert onto a lightly floured surface and knead well for about 10 minutes, or until smooth. Brush a bowl with oil. Shape the dough into a ball, place it in the bowl, and cover with a damp dish towel. Let rise in a warm place for 1 hour, or until the dough has doubled in volume. Preheat the oven to 425°F. Oil a 9-inch loaf pan. Invert the dough onto a lightly floured surface and knead for 1 minute, or until smooth. Shape the dough the length of the pan and three times the width. Fold the dough into three lengthwise and place it in the pan with the seam underneath. Cover and let rest in a warm place for 30 minutes, or until it has risen above the pan.

4. Place in the preheated oven and bake for 30 minutes, or until firm and golden brown. Test that the loaf is cooked by tapping the bottom with your knuckles—it should sound hollow. Transfer to a wire rack to cool.

3

3

Latticed Cherry Pie

 SERVES 8   PREP TIME: 40 minutes plus chilling   COOKING TIME: 45 minutes

nutritional information per serving	345 cal, 12.5g fat, 7.5g sat fat, 37g total sugars, 0.4g salt

This colorful pie is full of juicy cherries in a sweet almond- and cherry brandy-flavored syrup.

INGREDIENTS

pie dough
1 cup plus 2 tablespoons all-purpose flour, plus extra for dusting

¼ teaspoon baking powder

½ teaspoon allspice

½ teaspoon salt

¼ cup superfine sugar

4 tablespoons unsalted butter, chilled and diced, plus extra for greasing

1 egg, beaten, plus extra for glazing

filling
6 cups pitted fresh cherries (2 pounds), or 2 (15-ounce) cans cherries, drained

¾ cup superfine sugar

½ teaspoon almond extract

2 teaspoons cherry brandy

¼ teaspoon allspice

2 tablespoons cornstarch

2 tablespoons water

2 tablespoons unsalted butter, melted

ice cream, to serve

1. To make the dough, sift the flour with the baking powder into a large bowl. Stir in the allspice, salt, and sugar. Rub in the butter until the mixture resembles fine bread crumbs, make a well in the center, pour in the egg, and mix into a dough. Cut the dough in half, and use your hands to roll each half into a ball. Wrap in plastic wrap and chill in the refrigerator for 30 minutes.

2. Preheat the oven to 425°F. Grease a 9-inch deep pie plate. Roll out the doughs into two circles on a floured surface, each 12 inches in diameter. Use one to line the pie plate.

3. To make the filling, put half the cherries and all the sugar in a saucepan. Bring to a simmer and stir in the almond extract, brandy, and allspice. In a bowl, mix the cornstarch and water into a paste. Stir the paste into the saucepan, then boil until the mixture thickens. Stir in the remaining cherries, pour into the pastry shell, then dot with the melted butter. Cut the remaining dough circle into strips ½ inch wide. Lay the strips over the filling, crossing to form a lattice. Trim and seal the edges with water. Use your fingers to crimp around the rim, then glaze the top with the beaten egg.

4. Cover the pie with aluminum foil, then bake for 30 minutes in the preheated oven. Remove from the oven, discard the foil, then bake for an additional 15 minutes, or until golden. Serve with ice cream.

Sourdough Bread

MAKES
2 loaves

PREP TIME:
30 minutes plus
starter and rising

COOKING TIME:
30 minutes

nutritional information per loaf	1,302 cal, 23g fat, 5g sat fat, 49g total sugars, 10.3g salt

You'll need to plan ahead to make this rustic bread by preparing the starter dough a few days in advance.

INGREDIENTS

3¾ cups whole-wheat flour
4 teaspoons salt
1½ cups lukewarm water
2 tablespoons dark molasses
1 tablespoon vegetable oil, plus extra for brushing
all-purpose flour, for dusting

starter
¾ cup whole-wheat flour
⅔ cup white bread flour
¼ cup superfine sugar
1 cup plus 1 tablespoon whole milk

1. For the starter, put the whole-wheat flour, white bread flour, sugar, and milk into a nonmetallic bowl and beat well with a fork. Cover with a damp dish towel and let stand at room temperature for 4–5 days, until the mixture is frothy and smells sour.

2. Mix together the flour and half the salt into a bowl and add the water, molasses, oil, and starter. Mix well with a wooden spoon until a dough begins to form, then knead with your hands until it leaves the side of the bowl. Invert onto a lightly floured surface and knead for 10 minutes, or until smooth and elastic.

3. Brush a bowl with oil. Form the dough into a ball, put it into the bowl, and put the bowl into a plastic food bag or cover with a damp dish towel. Let rise in a warm place for 2 hours, or until the dough has doubled in volume.

4. Dust two baking sheets with flour. Mix the remaining salt with ¼ cup of water in a bowl. Invert the dough onto a lightly floured surface and punch down with your fist to knock out the air, then knead for 10 minutes. Halve the dough, shape each piece into an oval, and place the loaves on the prepared baking sheets. Brush with the salty water glaze and let stand in a warm place, brushing frequently with the glaze, for 30 minutes.

5. Preheat the oven to 425°F. Brush the loaves with the remaining glaze and bake for 30 minutes, or until the crust is golden brown and the loaves sound hollow when tapped on their bottoms with your knuckles. If it is necessary to cook them for longer, reduce the oven temperature to 375°F. Transfer to wire racks to cool.

Cinnamon Swirls

 MAKES 12   PREP TIME
1 hour
plus rising    COOKING TIME
20–30 minutes

nutritional information per pastry	170 cal, 8g fat, 5g sat fat, 9g total sugars, 0.3g salt

These homemade Danish pastries taste delicious warm, straight from the oven, for a mid morning treat.

INGREDIENTS

1⅔ cups white bread flour
½ teaspoon salt
2¼ teaspoons active dry yeast
2 tablespoons butter, cut into small pieces, plus extra for greasing
1 egg, lightly beaten
½ cup lukewarm milk
2 tablespoons maple syrup, for glazing

filling
4 tablespoons butter, softened
2 teaspoons ground cinnamon
¼ cup firmly packed light brown sugar
⅓ cup dried currants

1. Grease a baking sheet with a little butter.

2. Sift the flour and salt into a mixing bowl. Stir in the yeast. Rub in the butter with your fingertips until the mixture resembles bread crumbs. Add the egg and milk and mix to form a dough.

3. Form the dough into a ball, place in a greased bowl, cover with plastic wrap, and let stand in a warm place for about 40 minutes, or until doubled in size. Knead the dough for 1 minute, then roll out to a rectangle measuring 12 x 9 inches.

4. To make the filling, cream together the butter, cinnamon, and sugar until light and fluffy. Spread the filling evenly over the dough rectangle, leaving a 1-inch border all around. Sprinkle the currants evenly over the top.

5. Roll up the dough from one of the long edges, and press down to seal. Cut the roll into 12 slices. Place them on the baking sheet, cover, and let stand for 30 minutes.

6. Meanwhile, preheat the oven to 375°F. Bake the swirls in the preheated oven for 20–30 minutes, or until well risen. Brush with the maple syrup and let cool slightly before serving.

Bread Rolls

 MAKES 12 PREP TIME: 30 minutes plus rising COOKING TIME: 12–15 minutes

nutritional information per roll	173 cal, 7g fat, 4g sat fat, 2g total sugars, 0.3g salt

These crusty golden bread rolls are particularly good served warm with a steaming bowl of soup.

INGREDIENTS

½ cup whole milk

¼ cup water

5 tablespoons butter, softened, plus extra for brushing

2½ cups white bread flour, plus extra for dusting

2¼ teaspoons active dry yeast

1 tablespoon sugar

½ teaspoon salt

1 extra-large egg, beaten

sunflower oil, for greasing

1. Put the milk, water, and 2 tablespoons of the butter into a small saucepan and heat to 110–120°F. Put the flour, yeast, sugar, and salt into a large bowl, stir, and make a well in the center. Slowly pour in ⅓ cup of the milk mixture, then add the egg and beat, drawing in the flour from the side. Add the remaining milk, tablespoon by tablespoon, until a soft dough forms.

2. Grease a bowl and set aside. Invert the dough onto a lightly floured surface and knead for 8–10 minutes, or until smooth and elastic. Shape the dough into a ball, roll it around in the greased bowl, cover with plastic wrap, and set aside for 1 hour, or until doubled in size.

3. Invert the dough onto a lightly floured surface and punch down to knock out the air. Cover with the upturned bowl and let rest for 10 minutes. Meanwhile, preheat the oven to 400°F and dust a baking sheet with flour. Melt the remaining butter in a small saucepan over medium heat.

4. Lightly dust a rolling pin with flour and use to roll out the dough to a thickness of ¼ inch. Use a floured 3¼-inch round cookie cutter to cut out 12 circles, rerolling the trimmings, if necessary. Brush the middle of a circle with butter. Use a floured chopstick or pencil to make an indentation just off center, then fold along that indentation and pinch the edges together to seal. Place on the prepared baking sheet, cover with a dish towel, and let rise while you shape the remaining rolls.

5. Lightly brush the tops of the rolls with butter and bake in the preheated oven for 12–15 minutes, or until the rolls are golden brown and the bottoms sound hollow when tapped. Transfer to a wire rack to cool.

Apple Turnovers

 MAKES 8   PREP TIME: 40 minutes   COOKING TIME: 15–20 minutes

nutritional information per pastry	326 cal, 24g fat, 14g sat fat, 14g total sugars, 0.3g salt

Quick and easy to make, these sweet pastries are a great way to use up a bumper crop of apples.

INGREDIENTS

1 sheet ready-to-bake puff pastry (9 ounces), thawed, if frozen
flour, for dusting
milk, for glazing

filling
2 large cooking apples (about 1 pound), such as Granny Smith or Pippin, peeled, cored, and chopped
grated rind of 1 lemon (optional)
pinch of ground cloves (optional)
3 tablespoons sugar

orange sugar
1 tablespoon sugar, for sprinkling
finely grated rind of 1 orange

orange cream
1 cup heavy cream
grated rind of 1 orange and juice of ½ orange
confectioners' sugar, to taste

1. To make the filling, mix together the apples, lemon rind, and ground cloves, if using, but do not add the sugar yet because the juice will seep out of the apples. For the orange sugar, mix together the sugar and orange rind.

2. Preheat the oven to 425°F. Roll out the pastry on a floured surface into a 24 x 12-inch rectangle. Cut the pastry in half lengthwise, then across into four to make eight 6-inch squares.

3. Mix the sugar into the apple filling. Brush each square lightly with milk and place a little of the apple filling in the center. Fold over one corner diagonally to meet the opposite one, making a triangular turnover, and press the edges together firmly. Place on a baking sheet. Repeat with the remaining squares. Brush with milk and sprinkle with the orange sugar. Bake in the preheated oven for 15–20 minutes, or until browned. Let cool on a wire rack.

4. For the orange cream, whip together the cream, orange rind, and orange juice until thick. Add a little confectioners' sugar to taste and whip again until it just holds soft peaks. Serve the turnovers warm with orange cream.

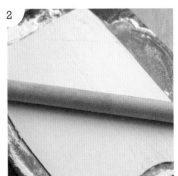

Cornbread

 MAKES
1 loaf

 PREP TIME:
15 minutes

 COOKING TIME:
30–35 minutes

nutritional information per loaf	3,247 cal, 171g fat, 89g sat fat, 19g total sugars, 12.8g salt

Cornmeal gives this yeast-free bread a wonderful golden color and distinctive flavor.

INGREDIENTS

vegetable oil, for greasing
1⅓ cups all-purpose flour
1 teaspoon salt
4 teaspoons baking powder
1 teaspoon superfine sugar
2 cups cornmeal
1 stick salted butter, softened
4 eggs
1 cup whole milk
3 tablespoons heavy cream

1. Preheat the oven to 400°F. Brush an 8-inch square cake pan with oil.

2. Sift together the flour, salt, and baking powder into a bowl. Add the sugar and cornmeal and stir to mix. Add the butter and cut into the dry ingredients with a knife, then rub it in with your fingertips until the mixture resembles fine bread crumbs.

3. Lightly beat the eggs in a bowl with the milk and cream, then stir into the cornmeal mixture until thoroughly combined.

4. Spoon the dough into the prepared pan and smooth the surface. Bake in the preheated oven for 30–35 minutes, or until a toothpick inserted into the center of the loaf comes out clean. Remove the pan from the oven and let cool for 5–10 minutes, then cut into squares and serve warm.

2

3

4

Coconut Cream Pie

 SERVES 6

 PREP TIME:
30 minutes
plus chilling

 COOKING TIME:
16–18 minutes

nutritional information per serving	753 cal, 62g fat, 37g sat fat, 12g total sugars, 0.6g salt

A simple pie crust filled with a layer of sweet coconut and vanilla pudding and topped with whipped cream and lightly toasted coconut.

INGREDIENTS

1 sheet store-bought rolled dough pie crust, thawed, if frozen
2 eggs
¼ cup superfine sugar
1 teaspoon vanilla extract
2 tablespoons all-purpose flour, plus extra for dusting
2 tablespoons cornstarch
⅔ cup whole milk
1 cup coconut milk
⅓ cup dry unsweetened coconut
1¾ cups heavy cream
2 tablespoons toasted dry unsweetened coconut, to decorate

1. Preheat the oven to 400°F. Roll the dough out on a lightly floured surface and use to line an 8–9-inch pie plate. Trim and crimp the edges. Prick the bottom with a fork and chill in the refrigerator for 15 minutes.

2. Line the pastry shell with parchment paper and pie weights or dried beans. Bake in the preheated oven for 10 minutes. Remove the paper and weights and bake for an additional 6–8 minutes, or until golden. Let cool.

3. For the filling, beat together the eggs, sugar, and vanilla extract in a bowl. Blend the flour and cornstarch to a paste with ¼ cup of milk, then beat the paste into the egg mixture. Heat the remaining milk and coconut milk in a saucepan until almost boiling and pour onto the egg mixture, stirring continuously. Return to the saucepan and slowly heat, beating until smooth and thick. Stir in the coconut. Cover with dampened wax paper and let stand until cold.

4. Spread the coconut filling in the pastry shell. Whip the cream until holding soft peaks and spread over the top of the filling. Sprinkle with the toasted coconut and serve.

Index